The Essence of Reiki

Usui Reiki Level 1 Practitioner Mar

A Complete Guide to the Usui Method of Natural Healing

by

Adele and Garry Malone

Reiki Masters/Teachers Since 1997

www.reiki-store.co.uk | www.reiki-store.com

© Copyright Notice

The Essence of Reiki 1
Usui Reiki Level 1 Practitioner Manual

Published by
GarryMalone.com Limited.
www.reiki-store.co.uk
www.reiki-store.com

Our Reiki Line Lineage

Dr Mikao Usui

Dr Chujiro Hayashi

Madam Hawayo Takata

Iris Ishikura

Arthur Robertson

Rick & Emma Ferguson

Margarette L Shelton

Kathleen Ann Milner

Robert N Wachsberger

Tricia Courtney-Dickens

Adele and Garry Malone

About the Authors

Adele and Garry Malone are highly experienced **Certified** Reiki Masters/Teachers, Life Coaches, Clinical Hypnotherapists and Master Practitioners of NLP who run a successful and busy practice from their Home Office and Healing Centre in Hertfordshire UK.

Since 1997 their combined practical Reiki experience and professional easy to follow books, workshops and home study courses, have offered the Reiki reader/student an holistic approach to the study, mastery and use of the USUI method of natural healing.

Adele and Garry have jointly authored a number of bestselling books, audio and visual programmes, certified home study courses and conduct Reiki and Personal Development workshops throughout the UK and Internationally.

Authors & Publishers Disclaimer

Reiki is an ancient form of healing that is practised by the authors and numerous practitioners around the world. The information and techniques in this book do not constitute medical advice. Healing and medicine are two very different disciplines. You should always remember to seek medical advice from a qualified doctor or practitioner in the case of serious illness. While all suggested treatments are offered in good faith, the author and publisher cannot accept responsibility for any illness arising out of the failure by the reader/individual to seek medical advice from a qualified doctor or medical practitioner.

Special Acknowledgement

Adele and Garry Malone would like to thank their Reiki Lineage especially Reiki Master **Tricia Courtney-Dickens**, for her wonderful ability to teach Reiki with such clarity and for passing on to them both this special gift of healing.

The Essence of Reiki 1 is **dedicated to our four wonderful children** Molly, Harriette-Rose, Charlotte and Garry.

In Memory
of
Kim Buckley

Important Note to the Reader

The purpose of this book is to give the reader a comprehensive guide to the teachings and disciplines associated with First Degree Usui Reiki. We have purposely kept the information concise so the reader can quickly and easily understand and apply Reiki.

Wherever possible we have avoided adding personal beliefs that may differ from the traditional teachings of Dr Mikao Usui. The knowledge and information contained in this book is based on the original **Shiki Ryoho** Method of Healing developed by **Dr Usui** over two hundred years ago.

If you desire to use the teachings contain within this book to heal yourself and others you must first have received the necessary attunements from a Reiki Master either in person or via distant attunement. You can find out how to become a Certified Usui Reiki Master Teacher with our Best Selling Reiki Master Video Home Study Course by visiting www.reiki-store.co.uk

"I am realistic. I expect miracles." - Dr. Wayne Dyer

Table of Contents

An Introduction to Usui Reiki

"To heal from the inside out is the key" – *Wynonna Judd*

Reiki is the gift of vitality and self preservation encoded into the genetic makeup of all God's creatures. It is the higher self's connection to the universal energy that breathes life into all living things. We are all born with the omniscient wisdom to heal and preserve life. All living things are connected. Our ancestors used and relied on their own abilities and instincts. Unfortunately, these basic skills have been forgotten and are rarely used today. Humanity in its relentless ambition for progress has given up its most precious and natural gift.

Through the media and clever advertising campaigns the majority of the world's population have been conditioned to rely heavily on modern technology at the expense of their own birthright. There is a need for humanity to become re-balanced. Instead of giving up responsibility for one's life and health, it is vitally important to regain equilibrium between ancient and modern technology. *Reiki is the catalyst*.

Many people believe when you are ready to embrace the principles of Reiki you will be guided to a teacher. I personally believe that Reiki with its infinite wisdom and unconditional love seeks out the person when they need it most. This is true of my own experience and introduction to Reiki.

Like many people in the healing profession I was inspired to help others through personal tragedy. My sister Kim Buckley died of Cancer at the young age of thirty-three, leaving behind a devastated husband, four young children and a large family. During her brief attempt to beat cancer she asked me to help her fight against this horrible disease. With no real knowledge of medicine or complementary therapies I searched for hope. Doctors and nurses were unable and unwilling to offer any encouragement, refusing to step outside the realms of modern medicine. We were told to just accept that she was going to die. Modern medicine gave up exposing its limitations.

Angry and frustrated at the hospitals' cold, blunt diagnosis I began to search bookshops for inspiration. Love, Medicine and Miracles a wonderful book by Dr Bernie Siegel jumped out at me. It told of a more compassionate and holistic approach to diseases such as cancer and aids. There were stories of people who survived even after being told there was no hope. It explained how by taking responsibility for your own health and future you could fight back if you wished. Even in death you could have control and dignity.

Dr Siegel, an oncologist had become disillusioned with the way he had been taught to treat his patients. After attending a seminar on guided imagery he decided to developed and pioneer an alternative approach. In 1978, Dr Siegel set-up a new therapy programme called ECAP (Exceptional Cancer and Aids Patients). Since then he has established centres throughout the USA. This book and Dr Siegel's work inspired me to change my life. My new path began with the study of the mind through Hypnosis and NLP (Neuro Linguistic Programming).

Fortunately for me, while I was training in Hypnotherapy and NLP I met a lady called Tricia Courtney-Dickens who introduced me to Reiki. Her enthusiasm for this ancient art of healing was infectious. I decided to enrol in her next Reiki course to study the first degree. That weekend workshop changed my perceptions of holistic healing. Reiki put me in touch with my natural abilities to heal myself and others; I was truly amazed by Reiki's subtle yet profound power.

"Eventually you will come to understand that love heals everything, and love is all there is" - Gary Zukav

1

Reiki the Universal Life Force

*Our sorrow and wounds are healed only when
we touch them with compassion – Buddha*

There is a non physical ubiquitous energy that gives life to every living organism. For many thousands of years we have known of this energy and have sought to develop ways to harness its power to heal and influence our lives. The Japanese call this energy Ki. It is also known as Chi by the Chinese, Prana by a number of Asian cultures and the Holy Spirit or Holy Ghost by most of the western world.

We carry this energy in and around our bodies from the moment we are conceived. Science has established its existence, and with the aid of Kirlian photography we are able to see this energy that encompasses all living things. Ancient Eastern cultures have harnessed and applied this energy for healing since before the birth of Jesus Christ.

Many successful disciplines such as Reiki, Tai Chi, Feng Shui, Meditation, Yoga and Acupuncture have been developed to control and greatly enhance the flow of this energy in and around the body. The energy itself is pure and has omniscient wisdom.

10 Things That Weaken the Life Giving Energy

Too much alcohol
A poor diet
A lack of exercise
Drugs
Tobacco
Negative habits
Stress
Poor breathing
A lack of sleep and rest
Negative psychic activity

Humanity has become fragmented and hollow; we are only a shadow of what we could be. We need to go back to go forward once more. By practising the discipline of Reiki you regain your natural abilities to heal yourself and others and the knowledge you require to lead a happier more fulfilling life.

Nature's life giving energy is a great and wise teacher, by pursuing its wisdom through Reiki you will grow to new heights of understanding and life will flow at a more enjoyable and exciting pace. Remember always that this life giving energy is a gift from God – your Birthright. Everyone possesses this gift and uses it daily even though they probably do not realise they are doing so.

When a child for instance falls and hurts their knee, instinctively they place their hand on the sore spot and the pain is relieved as they unconsciously work with this energy to heal them selves. Likewise, a parent will kiss their child's hurt or injured limb better and place their hand on top. Unknowingly both the parent and the child are working unconsciously with this healing energy. The parent is sending and channelling the energy; the child is receiving and drawing the energy.

This wonderful energy is free. There are no patents or copyrights attached. All you need is the desire and the discipline to attune yourself to the energy and its life changing properties.

A new philosophy, a way of life, is not given for nothing.
It has to be paid dearly for and only acquired with much patience and great effort.
- Fyodor Dostoyevsky

2

What is Reiki?

In the deeper reality beyond space and time,
we may be all members of one body - Sir James Jeans

Reiki is a form of hands on healing, with its origins in India and the East dating back many thousands of years to the time before Christ and Buddha. The original name, disciplines and techniques of Reiki were lost due to the traditional method of passing knowledge from generation to generation by word of mouth. Exactly when this ancient art of healing disappeared is difficult to determine. However, we do know that it was rediscovered by a Japanese Scholar and monk name Dr Mikao Usui. It was in fact Dr Usui who fashioned the name REIKI.

Rei - Universal

Ki - Life Force

Reiki is a two syllable Japanese word meaning universal life force. Although the proper Japanese pronunciation is RYE-KEY, it has been westernised to RAY-KEY.

Rei means universal, omnipresent – present everywhere at the same time. Esoterically Rei means spiritual consciousness, the omniscient wisdom from God or the higher self.

Ki is the non physical vitality that gives life to all living things. Many cultures understand and recognise the importance of Ki energy and how it impacts our lives and well-being.

Ki energy can be activated for the purpose of healing. When you feel healthy and full of enthusiasm, the flow of Ki energy in your body is high and unencumbered. Life seems easier to deal with and you have a higher resistance to illness and disease.

However, when your Ki energy is low because maybe you are under stress or feeling unhappy and tired you will be more susceptible to disease and sickness. Your attitude will be generally negative and you will find it difficult to deal with life's challenges. Ki is the very essence of the soul; it leaves the body when a person dies.

Reiki is holistic; it works on the body mind and spirit by stimulating a person's own natural healing abilities. The blocked emotional and physical elements that lead to illness and disease are cleared. Reiki is neither positive nor negative; it is in fact the highest and most profound vibration of life. Divine in origin, it allows us all to become one with all things alive in our world. Reiki is pure unconditional love and joy bringing all who experience and embrace it principles together in harmony.

The skills and techniques associated with Reiki are simple and easy to learn. Small children and adults can equally comprehend and incorporate this ancient form of healing into their lives. Regular contact with Reiki will bring the recipients mind body and spirit into balance. It will also help prevent future creation of illness and disease.

Reiki is the greatest secret in the science of energetic - Madam Hawayo Takata

3

How Reiki Works

You don't have a soul. You are a Soul. You have a body. ~ C.S. Lewis

The human body is made up of over 50 trillion cells. Each cell contains omniscient wisdom and is connected to the universe and every living thing within it. A good analogy is to think of the universe as a huge ocean of water. Every living thing within that ocean is like a tiny droplet. Together these droplets make up and are part of Reiki the universal life force.

Reiki is part of our genetic structure; an in built intelligence that energises the mind body and spirit. Reiki stimulates growth, health, life and healing. When it is freely allowed to flow around the body it can keep us alive and healthy for over one hundred and twenty years.

Unfortunately, bad habits and poor choices result in the flow of Reiki being stifled. It is important to note that Reiki cannot be destroyed. Even when we die and the life force leaves our body it continues to exist as part of the universe. Through neglect and ignorance we abuse this vital component of life.

When the mind body and spirit are in harmony the biological intelligence that governs the body's resources and allows it to heal itself and function correctly are intensified. Reiki is the key that unlocks the body's optimum capabilities. There are seven main energy centres in the body that control the flow of the universal life force. They are called the Chakra's. Each chakra is responsible for supplying energy to specific parts of the body. When they are blocked or clogged the body becomes sick and the flow of energy is diluted.

A full Reiki treatment reopens the chakras and re-balances the flow of the universal life force around the body. A person will normally need four full treatments on four consecutive days to boost the flow of Reiki energy. This will stimulate the body's immune system and natural healing abilities. Normally the body will begin by cleansing itself of toxins. As the poisons are removed, the body becomes re-balanced and the healing process can begin.

Many cultures have developed techniques and disciplines that stimulate the flow of KI energy around the body. However, Reiki is the easiest to learn and administer. The techniques are simple to master. The results are profound.

The 7 Major Chakra Points

1. **The Crown Chakra** (white or violet) is positioned on top of the head. It represents enlightenment, intuition and spiritual vision. Energy supplied to the pineal glands, upper brain and right eye.
2. **The Third Eye Chakra** (indigo) is positioned in the middle of the forehead, just above the eyebrows. It represents psychic perception, telepathy and ESP. Energy supplied to the spine, lower brain, left eye, pituitary gland, nose ears and central nervous system.
3. **The Throat Chakra** (light blue) is positioned in the centre of the neck. It represents self expression, emotions, communication and creativity. Energy supplied to the throat, thyroid gland, upper lungs, arms and digestive tract.
4. **The Heart Chakra** (rose and green) is positioned in the middle of the chest. It represents emotions, love, devotion, spiritual growth and compassion. Energy supplied to the heart, thymus gland, liver, lungs and the circulation system.
5. **The Solar Plexus Chakra** (yellow) is positioned just above the naval. It represents the centre of the body; food is assimilated, tuned into energy and distributed throughout the body. Energy supplied to the emotions, stomach, liver, digestion, gall bladder and the pancreas.
6. **The Sacral Chakra** (orange) is positioned just below the naval. It represents sexual energy, perceptions and the first impressions of people. Energy supplied to the reproductive organs, legs and the glands.
7. **The Root Chakra** (red) is positioned at the genitals. It represents life, physical vitality, birth and creation. Energy supplied to the spine, kidneys, bladder and the suprarenal glands.

Reiki is ever-present in our bodies. This means anyone can harness this profound inbuilt intelligent energy for healing.

However, without being attuned to the universal life force you will only be using about 10-20% of its capacity for healing.

Madam Takata explained it best when she described Reiki as being similar to radio waves. We cannot see them but we know they are everywhere around us. When we turn on a radio and tune into the radio waves we can pick up a signal. That signal is turned into a radio programme. Similarly the universal life force is everywhere, although we cannot see it unless we use Kirlian photography.

When we are tuned into the energy by a Reiki Master we are able to harness Reiki to heal ourselves and others. This gift of healing remains with us for the rest of our lives. We can only lose it if we use it for negative or destructive purposes. Reiki is pure and it needs to be treated as such.

Reiki is channelled through the hands. When you place your hands on your own body, or the body of another person for the purpose of healing you connect with the universal life force. The wisdom of Reiki then goes to work to bring about healing, balance and whatever is needed on a holistic level.

The best way to understand how Reiki works is to experience it.

God be in my head, and in my understanding.
God be in my eyes, and in my looking.
God be in my mouth, and in my speaking.
God be in my heart, and in my thinking.
God be at my end, and at my departing. – Anon

4

The History of Reiki

The best and most efficient pharmacy is within your own system - Robert C. Peale

The Japanese like many ancient cultures used word of mouth to pass their history and practices down from generation to generation. Unfortunately this led to a great deal of knowledge and wisdom being watered down and lost. Many people involved with Reiki believe that the techniques we use today for healing were first used in India by Buddha and later by Jesus.

Others look back even further to the civilisations of Mu and Atlantis for the birth and development of Reiki. Of course without written proof we can only speculate how humanity learnt to harness and develop the universal life force.

Dr Mikao Usui
Founder & 1st Grand Master

What we can be certain of and confirm is that it was rediscovered at the end of the nineteenth century by Dr Mikao Usui.

Until comparatively recently apart from the tomb of Dr Mikao Usui in Tokyo, there has been very little material evidence of his life and work. Most written accounts on the history of Reiki declare that Dr Usui was a Christian monk who lectured at Doshisha University in Kyoto. One day a student asked Dr Usui if he believed the teachings of the bible to be true. Could Jesus walk on water and heal people by touch. Audaciously he questioned if Dr Usui himself could heal the sick like Jesus.

Usui had to admit that this was beyond his capabilities. Embarrassed at being asked such questions and unable to demonstrate an answer, the story goes on to say that Doctor Usui immediately resigned his post and began a personal quest to discover how he could heal in the way that Jesus had. The legend becomes even more doubtful when it recounts how Dr Usui decided to begin his search for the secrets of healing like Jesus, in America – namely the University of Chicago.

Reiki Master William Rand has been able to disprove the legend of Dr Usui's search for enlightenment in America. Chicago University has no record of Dr Usui ever attending as a student. Furthermore there is no record of Dr Usui ever attending or lecturing at the Doshisha University. This work by William Rand confirms what many people believe. The history of Dr Usui's life had been changed and coloured to suit western society. Logically there are far too many holes in the legend.

The Life of Dr Mikao Usui

Mikao Usui was born into a family that had been practising Zen Buddhism for eleven generations. As a youth Usui developed a fascination for all things Western. However, he never travelled outside Japan. After leaving school he went on to study allopathic medicine with several western allopathic physicians who had graduated from Yale and Harvard University.

When a cholera epidemic spread through Tokyo, Usui was struck down with the disease. During his hospitalisation as he was close to death he had a spiritual experience. This inspired Usui to study the ancient teachings of his ancestors. He joined a Zen monastery and began reading the ancient Sanskrit and Sutras.

After many years of study Usui found references to an ancient form of healing. Further study revealed methods, formulas and symbols that detailed exactly how to practice and master this art of hands on healing. However, although he had the technical knowledge to practise healing, he lacked the wisdom to turn the teachings into reality. He needed the key to turn on and activate the power. Usui decided to seek the final piece of the jigsaw through meditation.

Taking leave from the monastery, Usui set off for the holy mountain of Kurama. When he reached the top he picked up twenty-one pebbles and placed them in front of himself. He sat down and began his meditation. Each day he threw away one pebble. For twenty-one days he prayed, meditated, sang and read the Sutras.

On the last day as he prayed he ask God to show him the light. Suddenly, a bright light appeared in the sky and came rapidly towards him, hitting him on his forehead, at the third eye chakra. Usui was knocked unconscious, and whilst in this altered state he saw a vision of the same symbols he had earlier found in the Sutras.

This vision was the confirmation Dr. Usui needed. He now knew that he had found the keys to the ancient form of healing used by Buddha and Jesus. When Usui regained full consciousness, he proceeded to return down the mountain. On his descent, he stubbed and cut his toe, he instinctively placed his hand on the toe and the bleeding and pain stopped.

On arrival at a nearby village he stopped to eat and rest. He was able despite having fasted for 21 days; eat a healthy meal without any stomach pain. The girl who served Usui the meal was in great pain suffering from a toothache. Usui asked if he could place his hands on her swollen face, she agreed, and he was able to ease the swelling and the pain. Rested, Usui returned to the monastery. On Arrival he found his friend, the Abbot in bed suffering with severe arthritis. Once again Usui was able to alleviate the pain and suffering. Usui called this gift from God – Reiki, the Japanese word for universal life force.

These experiences became known as the four miracles. Having demonstrated his knowledge and new ability to heal the Abbott advised Usui to take this special gift into the slums of Kyoto to heal the beggars. He was reminded that it is not enough to heal the body; it is of equal importance to heal the spirit and mind also. This lesson was brought home to him very abruptly seven years later. Having spent the time giving Reiki to beggars in the slums of Kyoto to get them working, he found them returning to him with the excuse that it was easier to beg.

Usui had forgotten a basic doctrine. Mortified he retreated to meditate once again. This time he was enlightened with the five principles of Reiki. The rest of Usui's life was spent healing, teaching and developing the Usui Shiki Rhoyo method of healing. Usui had nineteen major students who were all either western allopathic or traditional Japanese in their practice. He knew he would have to develop a method that could be understood and accepted by any religion or culture. Reiki was fashioned by Usui to have no dogma or religious beliefs attached to it. This made Reiki universal.

Tenno, the Emperor of Japan honoured Usui's work by awarding him a doctorate. By the time of his death in 1930, Dr Mikoa Usui had initiated all nineteen of his students to the level of Reiki Master/Teacher. Dr Chujiro Hayashi was chosen as the next Grand Master. It is important to note that Dr Usui taught all three degrees together. Dr Usui was cremated and his ashes placed in a Zen Monastery in Tokyo.

Dr Chujiro Hayashi

Dr Chujiro Hayashi
Second Grand Master

Upon the death of Dr Usui, Hayashi took over the role of Grand Master. He was responsible for training a further sixteen Reiki Masters and creating a set formula for training.

Chujiro Hayashi was born into an upper class Japanese family, and was a qualified physician and retired Marine commander.

He set up a clinic near the Emperors palace in Tokyo called Shina No Macha. Each day his students held healing sessions at the clinic, or visited people in their homes in they were unable to travel.

Hayashi went on to write many report on the systems he had developed to treat various ailments. Special diets were incorporated into his treatments to assist the healing process. Probably his greatest advancement for Reiki was to discover the importance of whole body treatment and how the universal life force would go wherever it was needed to heal. Providing of course you applied the full body treatment. This was needed to remove any emotional or physical blocks.

Madam Hawayo Takata

Madam Hawayo Takata
Third Grand Master

Hawayo Kawamuru was born on the Island of Hawaii on 24th December 1900. At the age of seventeen she married Saichi Takata.

They had a happy marriage with two daughters. Tragically, her husband died at the young age of thirty-two. After thirteen years of marriage Hawayo Takata was left to raise two small children on her own.

The stress and pressure of the situation took toll on her health. Within five years of her husbands' death she was diagnosed to be suffering from nervous exhaustion. Her health deteriorated to the point where she required surgery for a diseased gall bladder. However, she was also suffering from respiratory problems that meant the use of an anaesthetic during surgery could kill her.

This was an extremely depressing and trying time in her life. Unfortunately there was more pain and suffering to come when her sister died. As her parents had returned to live in Tokyo, it was Hawayo Takata traditional responsibility to bring the news to them in person.

After her arrival in Japan, she sought help at a hospital in Akasaka. It was discovered that she now had a tumour and appendicitis to add to her diseased gallbladder and respiratory problems. Her weight dropped dramatically and her doctor advised her to have immediate surgery.

That night as she lay in bed she heard a voice saying, "The surgery is not necessary." The next day as she was being prepared for surgery she heard the voice again saying, "The surgery was not necessary, ask - ask." Takata asked the surgeon if there was another way she could be healed and he told her of the Reiki clinic run by Dr. Hayashi. The surgeon had a sister who had been there herself and had recovered fully from an illness.

Madam Takata went to the clinic and received treatments regularly for four months and was completely healed. She decided that she also wanted to learn Reiki and set up her own practice in Hawaii. Against all tradition, she was eventually able to persuade Dr. Hayashi to allow her to work and train at the clinic for twelve months. At the end of this time it was felt that she had earned the privilege of receiving the second degree in Reiki – the advanced practitioners' level.

In the summer of 1937 Madam Takata returned to Hawaii and set up her own Reiki clinic. She spent her time healing and teaching Reiki. Dr Hayashi visited Madam Takata in February 1938 and invited her to become a Reiki Master. He said that she had gone through tests and had lived up to the Reiki Ideals and principles. She was the first woman and the first foreigner to be given this honour. Hayashi returned to Japan.

At the beginning of 1940 Japan was close to war with America. Dr Hayashi was aware he would be called up to fight. As a man of healing and peace he decided the only honourable thing to do was to precipitate his transition. He put his affairs in order. Madam Takata woke up one morning and saw a vision of Dr Hayashi at the foot of her bed. She realised she must travel immediately to Japan. On arrival in Japan she met with Dr Hayashi and he explained his decision to leave this world. They spent many days planning the future.

When Hayashi was satisfied he had safeguarded the future of Reiki he called all his students and friends together. At this point he declared Madam Takata his successor and the third Grand Master of Reiki. Dressed in traditional Japanese attire he lay down and allowed his spirit to leave his body. Madam Takata installed as the next Grand Master returned to Hawaii to continue her teaching and healing.

This is when the history of Reiki was changed to portray Dr Mikao Usui as a Christian. Madam Takata realised that the American people and the Western world in general would hold certain bigotry towards the Japanese. So soon after the War it would be impossible to promote a method of healing with its roots firmly in Buddhism and Japan.

Madam Takata went on to train a further twenty two Reiki Masters before her death in December 1980. There were two Grand Masters installed to continue Takata's work. Phyllis Lei Furumoto, the granddaughter of Madam Takata and Dr Barbara Weber. This partnership was to run for only a year until for personal reasons they split up to continue the work separately.

Phyllis Lei Furumuto
Fourth Grand Master

The Reiki Alliance was formed by Phyllis Lei Furumoto, while Dr Weber set up the A.I.R.A. (The American International Reiki Association).

Unfortunately, like many special things in this world the human ego has taken hold. There are now several different associations throughout the world all fighting amongst each other; each claiming to have the only correct way of teaching Reiki.

There is even a system of Reiki now being taught in eleven degrees. The latest rumours of an application to Copyright © Reiki seem to show how far this wonderful gift from God can be tainted.

There is only one Reiki. No-one has the right to claim it as their own, it belongs to humanity and the universe. Our only wish for the future of Reiki is that instead of fighting and bickering everyone involved with Reiki can again come together in the true spirit of healing.

Let's share our experiences and skills so Reiki can be accepted universally as a natural treatment for the mind body and spirit. We need to work together to promote this cause. It is vital in our increasingly harsh and violent world that we change the whole psyche of humanity.

Together we can bring this gift of healing to the world. We need Reiki practised and used in every hospital and clinic in the world. Let's spread the word positively. Let's make a difference. Let's make Dr Usui, Dr Hayashi and Madam Takata Proud. Let's honour their work and their memory. Let's live and internalise the Reiki Principles.

Although the world is full of suffering,
it is also full of the overcoming of it. - Helen Keller

5

The 5 Reiki Principles

Just for today I will not worry.
Just for today I will not be angry.
Just for today I will do my work honestly.
Just for today I will give thanks for my many blessings.
Just for today I will be kind to my neighbour and every living thing.

The Reiki principles are spiritual ideals. By adopting these precepts you will add balance and substance to your life. It is important that you realise that you are not expected to live every moment of your life within the framework of these ideals. As humans we are all imperfect, and that is why each principle begins with "Just for today." You can without pressure or stress work on improving yourself daily. If you slip up today, you can always begin again tomorrow. The more you work with the principles, the more you will condition yourself to adopt them as a way of life.

To become more familiar with the Reiki principles it is advisable to read them aloud at least twice a day. You may wish to place a large copy of the ideals in a picture frame. Then you could position the copy in a prominent place where you are sure to see it each day, or if you are going to practise Reiki professionally, place it in your healing room. The Five Reiki principles mean different things to each one of us. Meditation will help to unlock your own perceptions.

Simply sit or lie down in a comfortable position and close your eyes. Repeat one of the ideals several times aloud using it as a mantra. As you drift into a meditative state become aware of what happening inside your mind and body. You may experience many different feelings, emotions and thoughts. If you do this exercise in a group share your experiences and write down everything that happened during the meditation. It is interesting to look at your notes on this exercise on a regular basis to see how you have grown by adopting these precepts. Repeat the exercise of meditating on each principle annually and compare notes or if in a group setting discuss the differences that have taken place.

Just For Today I Will Not Worry

Worry causes stress and anxiety leading to an imbalance of the mind body and spirit and blockage to the root chakra.

The best way to overcome worry is to accept that all of us are faced with difficulties and setbacks in our lives. How we respond to them determines how we ultimately lead our lives.

If you choose to respond negatively by getting upset and anxious towards one of life's setbacks you have chosen to damage the balance of your mind body and spirit.

If you respond positively by accepting the setback as an opportunity to learn you can live a happier and more fulfilling life.

Allow yourself time each day to really laugh and have fun. Watch a funny movie or television show. Read a humorous book or magazine. Whatever it takes to make you laugh — do it. Ralph Waldo Emerson said, "Man surrounds himself with images of himself." This wonderful pearl of wisdom teaches us that if you want to be happy mix with happy people. Likewise if you want to be negative and constantly worrying you simple need to associate with people who are negative and worrisome.

Laughter is a wonderful healer. It has been proven through numerous studies that laughter can heal and in some cases prevent life threatening illnesses. Use this knowledge to live a healthier and longer life. Take responsibility for how you deal with life's setbacks. Have fun — life's too short to waste it worrying.

Use Reiki to re-balance your mind body and spirit and boost your resolve. Place one hand on the root chakra and the other hand on the heart chakra. Reiki will bring your mind body and spirit into equilibrium. Keep your hands over these chakra points for as long as you intuitively feel you need to. This Reiki technique will remove the blockages caused by stress, worry and anxiety. It can be used for self healing or on another person.

Just For Today I Will Not Be Angry

Just let go and relax

Anger is an emotion. When we get angry we lose control of that emotion. In order to live by the above principle we must understand what triggers our anger and how we can choose to remove this destructive emotion from our being.

In every confrontation that leads to anger the person or thing pushing your anger button has complete power and control over you.

This simple realisation allows you to take back control of your emotions and as such you can now choose to respond to a situation in a positive way rather than react to a situation in a negative way.

Every time you meet someone there is an exchange of energy. If you are both happy and find the meeting was enjoyable then the energy exchange is neutral. However, if you lose control of your emotions and become angry, the other person steals your energy. Likewise, if someone gets angry at you then you are stealing their energy.

With this simple philosophy you can counter the endless situations or people that in the past have triggered your anger and caused you to react in an unhealthy manner. Next time someone honks their car horn at you or criticises you for no apparent reason smile and say to yourself I am not going to let you steal my energy.

Just imagine how much better you will feel when you choose not to react to negative people or situations; how many times in the past have you shouted abuse at another car driver and still felt the anger in your stomach an hour or so later. That person stole your energy. They probably drove on laughing at how silly you looked when you lost your composure. You allowed them to cause you stress, anger and probably indigestion. Only one person came out of this confrontation with their energy intact and it wasn't you.

Anger is a choice response. Decide each day not to allow your energy to be stolen from you by negative people or situations. On a physical level anger can cause stomach and digestive disorders. Choose to live a healthier life free from anger.

Use Reiki to assist the re-balancing process. Place one hand on the third eye chakra and the other hand on the root chakra. Keep your hands there for as long as you intuitively feel is necessary. This Reiki technique will help you control and eliminate this destructive emotion. It can be used for self healing or on another person.

Just For Today I Will Do My Work Honestly

Honesty

Honesty means different things to different people. Many people feel it is fine to take home a few pens from the office, the company turn over millions in profit each year so they can afford to lose a few items of stationery.

While another person will judge the same incident as an act of theft and believe that anyone found stealing stationery should be dismissed and charged with theft and even prosecuted.

Everyone at some point is dishonest. You may not steal from another person or company, but instead steal from yourself.

For example if you a have a talent to help people and you choose not to then you are stealing from yourself by denying your gift.

You are also stealing from the people who could benefit from your talents. Wasting your time on meaningless pursuits such as watching television for hours each day is stealing from your sacred and special time on Earth. Try to live your life to the best of your ability as honestly as you can. Honesty lives inside of you and doesn't care about being placed where others can view it.

Finally, in your pursuit of a happier life I urge you to encapsulate the words from Michael Landon (the father in the television series "Little house on the Prairie") in his last interview before he died prematurely of cancer. He urged us to "Live Every Second".

Place one hand on the third eye chakra and the other hand on the solar plexus chakra to use Reiki to assist in the re-balancing of this principle. Keep your hands there for as long as you intuitively think they need to remain on these chakra points. This additional hand position can be used for healing yourself or other people.

"Honesty is the best policy."- Richard Whately, Archbishop of Dublin

Just For Today I Will Give
Thanks For My Many Blessings

Life tends to give us what we need, it may not be what we want but it will be what we need. Karmicly throughout our lives we receive what we need to grow and learn in this lifetime.

If we grasp these lessons and grow accordingly we will become spiritually enlightened. Instead of wasting your life complaining of the things that have happened to you, and the problems you face.

Step back for a moment on a regular basis and discover and appreciate the many blessings in your life.

Make a list of all your blessings. You will be amazed at how many wonderful things there are to give thanks for. Leave the materialistic things aside. They are shallow and meaningless. Pay attention to, and focus on the things that are free and bring joy and humility to your life. For example, your mind, body, spirit, health, family, friends, flowers, trees, sea, sun, love, faith, knowledge, the countryside, animals, birds, etc., the list is endless.

When you appreciate the true wonders of life and let go of the materialistic things you are bound to enjoy your life more.

Place one hand on the third eye chakra and the other hand on the occipital ridge. Use Reiki to re-balance this principle in your life or in the life of another person.

Just For Today I Will Be Kind to
My Neighbour and Every Living Thing

The law of karma states that what goes around comes around. Send out love and you will receive love back in return. Send out kindness and you will receive kindness. Send out healing and you receive healing. Send out positive thoughts and you will receive positive results.

Karma is a two edge sword. Send out negative thoughts and you will get negative results. Living within this precept will give you a happier and less stressful life full joy peace and love.

To bring balance to this principle for yourself or others first place one hand on the third eye chakra and the other hand on the root chakra. When you feel you are ready, move your hand from the third eye chakra to the throat chakra, and move your hand from the root chakra to the heart chakra keeping it there until you intuitively feel you have finished.

*It is important to remember that **the Reiki principles are only guides** for a happier and more fulfilling life. Use meditation to unlock the true meaning of these precepts and incorporate them into your life. They will tranceform your life.*

The 5 Reiki Principles are not commandments; they are simply gifts of wisdom.

Healing yourself is connected with healing others. - Yoko Ono

6

Preparing For Reiki 1

The art of healing comes from nature, not from the physician. Therefore the physician must start from nature, with an open mind. - Philipus Aureolus Paracelsus

The Path to Reiki

People from all walks of life are drawn to Reiki for many different reasons. Many people come to Reiki after a personal recommendation from a friend who has already attended a workshop. They notice positive changes in their friend and decide to experience it for themselves. A large majority of people simply need healing and want to take responsibility and control of their own treatment and well-being. The most common factor seems to be that people are searching for hope and guidance. Often people feel empty and are looking for a way of filling that void.

Many students begin as sceptics just curious to find out more about it, and leave as Reiki enthusiasts. The secret to getting the most from Reiki is to be open to Reiki. Instead of being negative and sceptical let the joy of Reiki envelop you. Leave your fears and doubts behind and jump head first in to a life changing experience. Reiki draws you to itself. If you are attending a seminar / workshop on first degree Reiki, you are there for a reason — you need it. Trust in the omniscient wisdom of Reiki. Remember you will only need the First Degree attunement once in your life, so make it a celebration you will never forget. It's up to you.

The Initiation Ceremony

In order to work with, and become a channel for Reiki you need to go through the first degree initiation ceremony, which consists of four attunements. These attunements are normally done over the course of a two day workshop. I prefer to do the four attunements at the same time as I believe it is beneficial to the student. The energy is stronger and the student is able to work and practice at their full capacity throughout the workshop. This process also allows the student to feel sense and experience more of the Reiki energy.

The four attunements are given on both days of the workshop, to supercharge the student and raise their energy vibration to the peak level possible with first degree Reiki. We also offer a distant attunement service as part of this home study course; please click here for more information.

Preparing for the Workshop

Before attending the first degree workshop there are a few basic things you should do in preparation. These guidelines will enable you to get the most from the workshop and the Initiation ceremony.

Avoid taking alcohol or any other form of drug for at least forty-eight hours before the workshop. These substances slow and hinder the flow of Reiki throughout the body.

Avoid eating meat, fish, processed foods or any other junk food for at least twenty-four hours. If possible have a day of fresh fruit, salad and vegetables. The digestion of food takes more energy than any other bodily function. Proteins and highly processed foods take more time to digest and will steal vital energy from your body.

If possible meditate each day for a week before attending the workshop. This will help to focus your thoughts, expectations and mind on becoming a Reiki channel for healing.

The Morning of the Workshop

Get up earlier than normal so you have plenty of time to prepare for the day ahead. You will then have time to relax and not become rushed or stressed.

If possible take a walk or a gentle jog to energise your system.

Avoid tea or coffee. However, naturally caffeine free herbal tea is fine.

Eat only fruit for breakfast. You will have more energy for the workshop.

Mentally prepare yourself with a short meditation.

Give yourself plenty of time to reach your destination. The stress of being late can upset your day and your enjoyment.

Come to the workshop with an open mind body and spirit. You will get out only what you put into the workshop.

What Happens During The Initiation?

Many people wonder why the initiation ceremony must remain a secret and why the students need to close their eyes during the attunements. Questions like these are quite normal, and understandable. The reason for the secrecy is to keep the rituals sacred and cherished by the Reiki Master and their students. The eyes kept closed allow the recipient being attuned to go inside and focus on the experience, it also helps the Reiki Master concentrate on what is a complex set of procedures.

During the initiation, the Reiki Master uses the ancient symbols and mantras (holy words that activate and direct certain energies) rediscovered by Dr. Usui to connect the student to the universal life force.

Dr. Hayashi described it to Madam Takata so beautifully when he said, "the universal life force is so big we cannot measure it, so deep we cannot fathom it; therefore in Japanese we call it Reiki." He continued "it is comparable to a radio station, broadcasting radio waves everywhere. There are no wires connecting the radio station with your home, yet when you turn on the receiver and tune into the radio waves from the station you receive what they are sending. Likewise, the principles of Reiki are the same. The energy is everywhere; it travels through space without wires. Once you have been connected to the energy it flows automatically, forever. It is a universal and immeasurable energy and its power is unlimited."

What Happens After Initiation?

When you receive your first attunement during the initiation ceremony, energy will start to flow through your hands at the thought of healing. You will also start a 21 day cleansing and detoxification cycle through the chakras. The Reiki attunement has a powerful healing influence on the mind body and spirit, activating all seven chakra's, beginning with the root, and ending at the crown chakra — each one taking approximately twenty-four hours. This happens three times.

You may not be aware of this depending on how fit and healthy you are. The more toxic you are the more you will be aware of the cleansing process. Your body is preparing you for healing. When the toxins are out of your system your body can work at its ultimate level for healing. Your whole system will be readjusted and re-balanced. You may experience symptoms of physical cleansing and detoxification such as a running nose, headaches or diarrhoea. There is no need to be alarmed the body is simply flushing out the toxins. It is a good idea to spend a bit more time resting over the twenty-one day period; use the time for self healing and reflection.

Place your hands on any aches or pains you may be experiencing and allow Reiki to ease your discomfort and speed up the healing process.

The healing energy works on all levels of the mind body and spirit. This process can be quite emotional and exhausting at times as the Reiki energy goes to work on the emotional and physical blocks, scars and baggage that your body has collected and stored throughout your lifetime.

Reiki's wisdom will do whatever is needed to release you from the fears and barriers that prevent you leading a happy fulfilling life. If you find yourself getting emotional and wanting to cry, scream or shout, let it happen. The old saying better out than in is so true and therapeutically beneficial to your being. Release the ties that bind you to your old habits and lifestyle. Reiki is like a rebirth. You can cleanse your mind body and spirit and start again. Trust in the healing power of Reiki.

Some reactions may seem unpleasant but by accepting them as part of your personal healing process and not attaching a great deal of importance to them, they will soon pass. You may also find yourself dealing with certain issues in your dreams; it can be helpful to keep a record of them in a dream journal. Then when you have time you can meditate on the issues. There are also two extremely good techniques for unravelling the meanings of dreams and how they relate to your life.

The first is 'Dreamwork' which is a form of Gestalt therapy developed by Dr Fritz Perls. It is simple and easy to understand. You are shown how to conduct conversations with your dreams. During these conversations your unconscious mind will unlock and reveal the true meaning of your dreams to you. There are many good books on this subject including The Red Book of Gestalt by Gaie Houston.

Professor Eugene Gendlin developed another technique for working with your dreams called Focussing. This subtle yet profound skill teaches you how to get in touch with the wisdom of the body. Ann Weiser Cornell's excellent book The Power of Focusing is a practical guide to using Professor Gendlin's techniques to unravel the meanings of your dreams.

The attunements 'switch on' an extra surge of power which fuels all life. The more you use Reiki the stronger it becomes. Establish the habit of giving yourself Reiki before you fall asleep at night and when you wake up in the morning. Remember, once you have been attuned to the universal life force you can begin channelling the healing energy of Reiki to yourself and others.

Reiki is never sent, it is always drawn through the channel. This is one of the major differences between Reiki and magnetic or spiritual healing. Because the energy is drawn through the channel by the recipient as opposed to being directed by the healer, the Reiki practitioner will never feel drained or take on the condition of the patient. On the contrary, the practitioner is also receiving a self – treatment as the Reiki energy flows through them to the recipient.

Your psychic, intuitive and creative abilities will be raised by between 50 to 80 percent. By raising your vibratory level you will begin a Tranceformational process on all the many levels and aspects of your life.

We all live in an extremely stressful and hectic world, which can influence our total being. Reiki helps control how our mind body and spirit responds both internally and externally to the often negative and destructive external stimuli from our world. If applied regularly, Reiki will reduce the extreme highs and lows of life, gradually leading to a new balanced existence.

Ways to Use Reiki after the Attunement

Once you have been attuned to Reiki, the energy will flow through your hands whenever you touch with the intention of healing or helping. You can use Reiki on:

- Yourself
- Other Adults (Family, Friends, Colleagues, Clients)
- Children
- Prenatal babies
- Accident Patients/Situations
- Emergency Situations
- Animals
- Birds
- Insects
- Fish
- Plants, Trees, Seeds and Your Garden
- Crystals
- Food (During preparation or before you eat)
- Drinks
- Your Work or Career
- Contracts or Contract Negotiations
- Projects
- Letters and Important Documents
- Your Car, Motorbike or Cycle
- For protection in general or when you are travelling
- Your Home or Office
- Drinking Water
- Bath or Shower Water

The practice of forgiveness is our most important contribution
to the healing of the world. - Marianne Williamson

7

Anatomic Illustrations for Reiki

There is something beautiful about all scars of whatever nature. A scar means the hurt is over, the wound is closed and healed, done with. - Harry Crews

Reiki with its infinite wisdom goes to the place in the body that requires healing. That is why Reiki is so easy to learn and apply. There is no need to study the anatomy of the human body or animals to treat a person or animal successfully. You simply place your hands on the body and channel the energy. Reiki will do the rest.

However, it can be helpful to know where the major organs, lymphatic and endocrine systems are in the body. This knowledge will allow you to treat specific problems or organs quickly and easily.

The following illustrations are simple diagrams of the human anatomy. If you decide to further your studies we recommend that you make full use of your public library. They will have books on the Human anatomy as well as books on the anatomy of various pets and animals. Of course the internet and the World Wide Web offer a multitude of FREE information and any good search engine will open up a doorway to many excellent guides to the anatomy.

The Endocrine System

This system consists of the ductless glands that release hormones. It works together with the nervous system in regulating metabolic activities so that homeostasis is maintained.

There are a few primary endocrine glands:

- The pituitary gland at the base of the brain

- The thyroid gland in the neck

- The four or five parathyroid glands in the tissue around the thyroid

- The two adrenal glands above the kidney against the posterior wall of the abdomen

- Certain areas of the pancreas near the stomach

- The sex glands, or gonads (testes in the male and ovaries in the female)

Various hormones are released by the endocrine glands, with each secretion causing a different reaction in the body. These include the body's growth rate, control of sex and reproductive functions, and the regulation of calcium and phosphate levels in the blood.

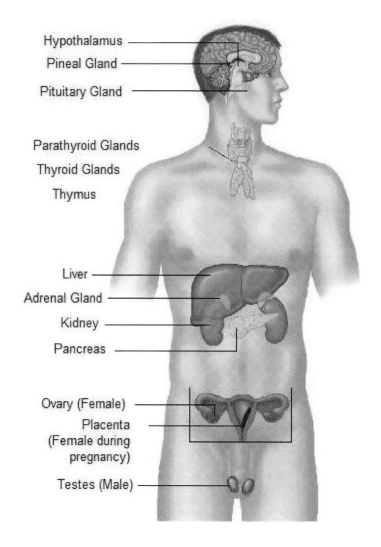

The Major Body Organs

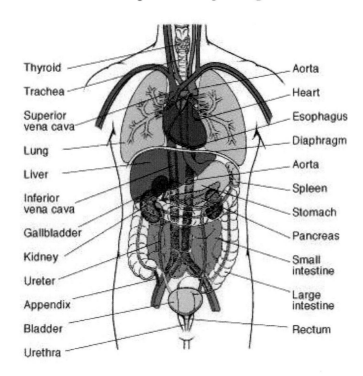

Thyroid
Trachea
Superior vena cava
Lung
Liver
Inferior vena cava
Gallbladder
Kidney
Ureter
Appendix
Bladder
Urethra

Aorta
Heart
Esophagus
Diaphragm
Aorta
Spleen
Stomach
Pancreas
Small intestine
Large intestine
Rectum

The Lymphatic System

The lymphatic system is a system of thin tubes that runs throughout the body. These tubes are called 'lymph vessels'. You may also hear them called 'lymphatic vessels'.

The lymphatic system is similar to blood circulation – the tubes branch through all parts of the body like the arteries and veins that carry blood. Except that the lymphatic system carries colourless liquid called 'lymph'.

"Lymph" is a milky body fluid that contains a type of white blood cells, called "lymphocytes," along with proteins and fats. Lymph seeps outside the blood vessels in spaces of body tissues and is stored in the "lymphatic" system to flow back into the bloodstream. Through the flow of blood in and out of arteries, and into the veins, and through the lymph nodes and into the lymph, the body is able to eliminate the products of cellular breakdown and bacterial invasion.

Two very large areas are of significance in this system – the right lymphatic duct which drains lymph fluid from the upper right quarter of the body above the diaphragm and down the midline, and the thoracic duct, a structure roughly sixteen inches long located in the mediastinum of the pleural cavity which drains the rest of the body. It is through the actions of this system including the spleen, the thymus, lymph nodes and lymph ducts that our body is able to fight infection and to ward off invasion from foreign invaders.

Lymph plays an important role in the immune system and in absorbing fats from the intestines. The lymphatic vessels are present wherever there are blood vessels and transport excess fluid to the end vessels without the assistance of any "pumping" action. There are more than 100 tiny, oval structures (called lymph nodes). These are mainly in the neck, groin and armpits, but are scattered all along the lymph vessels. They act as barriers to infection by filtering out and destroying toxins and germs. The largest body of lymphoid tissue in the human body is the spleen.

I just refer to myself as being Spirit, Mind and Body like everybody
else and working toward the mastery of my natural divinity
and the healing of my emotional mind. - Leonard Orr

8

Reiki Self Treatment

It is reasonable to expect the doctor to recognize that science may not have all the answers to problems of health and healing. - Norman Cousins

Once you have received the first degree attunement, from a Reiki Master you are ready to work with the universal life force. However, it is important that you realise as with every profession there is a need to first practice and master the skills associated with healing. Madam Takata taught her students to heal themselves first, then their families, then their friends. Only then did she believe they would be adequately qualified and able to work as a practitioner and heal other people.

When a person first learns to drive a car they need time, practice and experience to master what appears to be a rather complex set of procedures. However, within a relatively short space of time they can drive safely and effortlessly as they unconsciously control the car and all the various skills associated with driving.

Likewise with time, practice and experience you will master the skills and techniques associated with art of Reiki healing. Treat the early months as a learning experience, almost like an apprenticeship; this will give you the time you need to develop your confidence and skills. Remember the more you work with Reiki the more intuitive you will become, your energy vibration will be raised and you will develop and experience a new joyful consistency in your life.

Self healing is the starting point for personal development and self discovery. Reiki is not just a tool for healing; it also brings protection, prevention and personal transformation on all levels. As you progress along your new path, inevitably you will come up against obstacles and setbacks in your life that often seem like the whole ocean front, but with Reiki you will have the strength to deal with them as though they are but pebbles on the beach. Even if you never use Reiki to heal anyone but yourself, you will find a new sense of balance and peace in your life.

There is no other method of self-treatment as simple and as effective as Reiki. Because Reiki is always available to you, whenever you feel tired, stressed, have any aches or pains, you can alleviate them by simply laying your hands on your body. The infinite wisdom of Reiki will go to wherever it is needed.

Recharge your batteries every day, not just when problems, difficulties, anxiety or illnesses arise. Daily self treatment will help to prevent sickness and disease, and bring your life into focus and balance quickly. Every time you use Reiki on yourself, you raise your self esteem and self love. You will discover your mission in life and become more compassionate and loving.

Instead of getting stressed at the normal things you come into contact with each day such as traffic jams; meetings, interviews, going to the doctor's or dentist, waiting in queues, your children needs and your family responsibilities to name but a few, allow Reiki into your life and let Reiki become a new way of life to you.

Set aside a little time each day for a self treatment. First thing in the morning will give you a positive boost for the day ahead. Alternatively, a self treatment last thing at night will relax and unwind you, leading to a good night's sleep. Good places for a self-treatment are in the bath, the shower, or lying in bed. The possibilities are endless and the benefits are immeasurable.

Reiki is a gift to be savoured and enjoyed. Remember the more you use Reiki the stronger and more profound it becomes. Daily use could extend your own life by a number of years.

HOW REIKI CAN HELP YOU

There are a number of benefits to be gained, which occur without any effort from a daily Reiki self-treatment including:

- Reiki will relax you when you are stressed
- Reiki brings about deep relaxation
- Reiki centres your thoughts when you are confused
- Reiki energises you when you feel drained
- Reiki calms you when you are frightened
- Reiki focuses your mind and helps you to solve problems
- Reiki relieves pain
- Reiki accelerates natural healing of wounds
- Reiki improves health
- Reiki gradually clears up chronic problems
- Reiki helps prevents the development of disease
- Reiki detoxifies the body
- Reiki dissolves energy blockages
- Reiki releases emotional wounds
- Reiki increases the vibrational frequency of the body
- Reiki helps change negative conditioning & behaviour

HOW TO TREAT YOURSELF WITH REIKI

There is no right or wrong way to work with Reiki on oneself. As you become more experienced with the Reiki energy you will intuitively move your hands to wherever it feels right. However, if you are aware of a specific problem such as an injury or pain, then you should place your hands directly over that area to begin with, and follow up with a full self treatment.

In the beginning, it is always best to follow a set procedure as shown in the following illustrations marked "Self Treatment Hand Positions".

When you have mastered the hand positions you can then leave each self treatment up to your own intuition. You may wish to work with music to add the right relaxing mood. Find a place where you won't be disturbed if possible. Normally you would spend three to five minutes on each position.

However time is often short; but remember *a little Reiki is better than no Reiki*. On completion of the self treatment drink a large glass of purified water. Close your eyes and go inside and pay attention to the thoughts and emotions that have arisen during the session. You may feel light headed, and if you need to rest, or sit down for a short time, allow yourself this time.

If you feel you need to continue to work on a specific area of the body, even if you have completed a full self treatment, then go with your intuition; always listen to your mind and body.

Remember the following hand positions are only a guide – *Use your intuition*

SELF TREATMENT HAND POSITIONS

Hand Position 1

Cup your hands and gently rest them over your eyes, cheekbones and forehead (third eye chakra).

Stress, eye problems, asthma, head colds, allergies, sinuses, pituitary gland, pineal gland and cerebral nerves.

Hand Position 2

Place your hand on top of your head with fingertips touching (crown chakra).
Migraine, headaches, eye problems, multiple sclerosis, stress, bladder, digestive
disorders, flatulence and emotional problems.

Hand Position 3

Hands on either side of your head with fingers covering your temples.
Balance, tinnitus, balance and ear problems, colds, flu and balances the function
of the right and left brain.

Hand Position 4

Place your hands on the back of your head covering the occipital ridge.

Headaches, eye problems, stress, hay fever, sinuses, digestive disorders, fears, phobias, shock depression and stroke.

Hand Position 5

Hands covering the top of the shoulders and the bottom of the neck.

Aches and pains, stress, neck, tight muscles, nerves, spinal injury and shock.

Hand Position 6

Place your hands around the neck with the heels covering the throat (throat chakra).

Self expression, communication, breathing, voice and speech problems, bronchitis, flu, colds and anger.

Hand Position 7

Hands form a T, left hand covering the heart (heart chakra) & the right hand over the thymus gland.

Heart, angina, lungs, thymus, thyroid, weight problems, immune system, lymph, emotional problems and stress.

Hand Positions 8 - 11

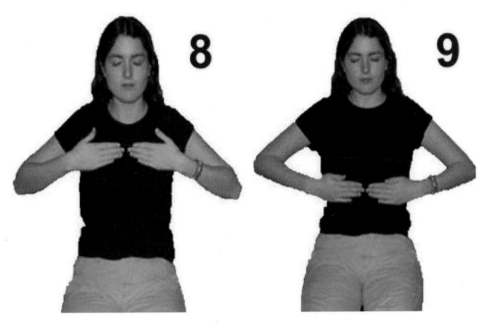

Position 8 the hands are positioned horizontally at the top of the torso just above the chest/breasts.

Position 9 the hands are positioned horizontally just below the chest/breasts.

All major organs and glands, disease, infections, stomach, intestines, reproductive organs, anger and emotions.

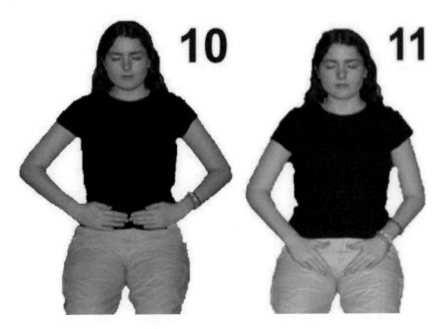

Position 10 the hands are positioned horizontally at the centre of the stomach.

Position 11 the hands are positioned in a V inside the hip bone.

All major organs and glands, disease, infections, stomach, intestines, reproductive organs, anger and emotions.

Hand Positions 12 and 13

Position 12 the hands are placed over the front of the knees.

Position 13 the hands are placed behind the back of the knees.

As an alternative method you can also cup both hands around the right knee first (position 12) and then cup both hands around the left knee if you find this more comfortable.

Leg pains, varicose veins, mobility issues and poor circulation.

Hand Positions 14 - 17

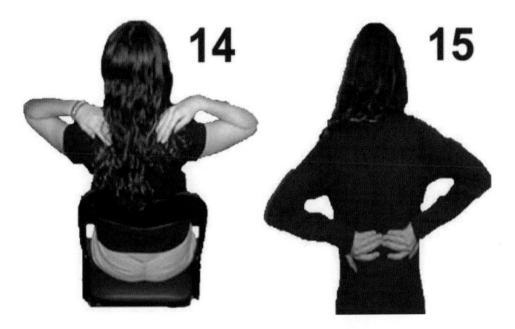

Position 14 the hands are positioned on top of the shoulders.

Position 15 the hands are positioned horizontally as high up the back towards the bottom of the shoulder blades as possible/comfortable.

All major organs and glands, disease, infections, back and spinal problems and stress.

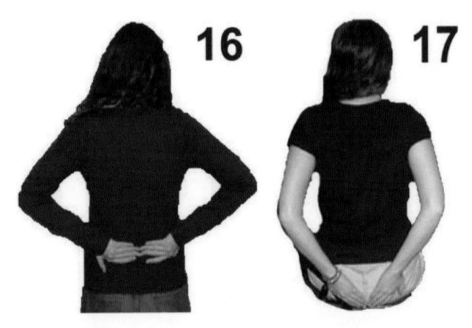

Position 16 the hands are positioned horizontally at the lower back area just below the back of the rib cage.

Position 17 the hands are positioned in a V at the base of the spine.

All major organs and glands, disease, infections, back and spinal problems and stress.

Hand Position 18

Sit in the lotus position and hold both feet with your hands.

Alternatively, if this position is too uncomfortable, you can sit cross legged with your right leg resting on your left leg and place your hands on the top and underside of your right foot, and then alternate and place you're your hands on the top and underside of your left foot as it rests on your right leg.

Leg pains, varicose veins, all major organs and glands (reflexology points).

The cure for pain is in the pain. - Roger Woolger

9

Preparing To Treat

Others with Reiki

Love one another and help others to rise to the higher levels, simply by pouring out love. Love is infectious and the greatest healing energy. - Sai Baba

Appropriate Environment

It is important to create the right setting whenever possible for a Reiki healing session. You may work from home and be able to use a spare room just for healing. If this is not practical you may want to look at the viability of joining your local therapy/healing centre. In most cases you will be able to rent a healing/therapy room at a reasonable hourly/daily/weekly basis.

The room should be light and clean, and feel safe. Bright pastel colours such as white, yellow or purple can be used to create the desired effect. Make sure you will not be interrupted by internal or external distractions, so unplug the telephone and disconnect the doorbell. If you're working from home let your family or friends know your schedules so they do not disturb you.

If possible always use a therapy table. Alternatively, you could use a strong table with thick blankets on top. You will need two pillows, one for the clients head and other for their feet. Make sure the room is heated to a comfortable level. Some people may get cold just lying still on your treatment table so always have a warm blanket available.

Add a plant to the room and some crystals under the table to help with the right energy. Some people like to work in total silence during a session. Personally we prefer to always work with therapeutic music such as classical, ambient or new age to help our clients relax. Music also can help the therapist relax and allow them to focus on healing. Natural sounds such as whales, dolphins and running water are very therapeutic and relaxing.

As part of our Distant Attunement service we also provide you with our own specially composed music for healing and meditation called 'Heartbeat' which is extremely relaxing and therapeutic, and a beautiful guided meditation based on the ancient light meditation.

We recommend you play this music while you treat other people and yourself with Reiki. There are also a wide range of compact discs and tapes available that have been created specifically for Reiki. They have been designed to run for the length of a full treatment with a bell or chime added at three or five minute intervals to let the therapist know when to move their hands to another position.

Burning incense or oils can add a pleasing aroma to your room. However, be careful as some people are sensitive to certain smells and it may cause them to experience an unpleasant therapy session. To prevent this happening ask your client before you light your oils or incense sticks. During a Reiki session you may find your client begins to cry as they release blocked emotional issues, so always keep a box of tissues handy for these occasions.

For a finishing touch to your room you may want to place photographs of Dr. Usui, Dr. Hayashi, Madam Takata, Buddha or Jesus, depending on who you call upon during your invocation / prayer.

Remove All Jewellery

Reiki can travel through all materials such as stone, brick, concrete and metal. However, the metal and stones used in the manufacture of jewellery come into contact with and attract certain types of negative energy. To enable you to work with Reiki free from all subtle energy disturbances it is advisable to remove all jewellery such as rings, watches, earrings, chains and necklaces.

Therapist's who work with precious stones and crystals for healing recognise that these materials can become saturated with negative energy. That is why they cleanse them on a regular basis.

Remove Tight Clothing

To allow Reiki to flow freely through you and your client it is important that you both remove tight clothing such as belts, ties and shoes. This will also make you feel more comfortable and relaxed. Reiki can travel through clothes so there is no need to remove any other forms of clothing. You may find it more comfortable if you wear loose fighting clothes when you are working with Reiki such as a tracksuit.

Avoid Alcohol

Alcohol dissipates energy. Always refrain from consuming alcohol if you know you are going to be working with Reiki for at least twenty-four hours before a session.

Personal Hygiene

Ensure you smell and appear clean and fresh. Avoid wearing strong perfumes or after shaves. If you smoke make sure you brush your teeth or use a mouth freshener. Refrain from eating garlic, onions or any other food that may leave a smell on your breath.

Wash your hands before a Reiki session using a lightly scented or neutral soap. Your hands come into contact with your clients face and skin so it is important for hygiene purposes and the peace of mind of your client to have clean hands.

The Invocation

It is important to remember that as a Reiki practitioner you are not healing your clients. The people receiving Reiki are in fact healing themselves. You are merely the channel that enables them to draw the Reiki energy through your hands to the place it is needed. The invocation is a token that symbolises you are giving up any claims to power. You are simply the conduit in which the infinite power of the universal life force flows.

Although the invocation is not necessary to turn on the Reiki energy I feel it enables the therapist to disassociate themselves from their ego and pay respect to the universal life force and the person they are about to work with.

Your prayer should be personal and in line with your own beliefs. Ask for permission to be used as a channel for Reiki healing. We have listed below our own personal invocation which may help you develop a prayer that is suitable for your own use.

Once your client is lying down on the healing table; relaxed and ready to receive Reiki move to the top the table (the clients head). Close your eyes and join your hands together in a prayer like position in front of your heart chakra. Alternatively, if your client is seated, place your hands on their shoulders for the invocation.

Garry and Adele Malone's Personal Invocation

We always like to take a few moments before we begin a treatment to mentally prepare ourselves for working as a channel for Reiki. This quiet time is perfect for getting in touch with our guides, mentors and assistants. It allows us a brief moment of reflection and focuses our thoughts on healing. It is important to begin the treatment with the right mental attitude. Your wish should be to pass on unconditional love and healing in the purest form and sense.

"I call upon Reiki – the Universal Life Force, all the Angelic beings who have work with Reiki in the past especially Dr. Usui, Dr. Hayashi, Madam Takata, my guides and all the Reiki Masters past, present and future to draw near and take part in this healing session.

I ask that the power and wisdom of Reiki permits me to become a channel for Reiki's unconditional love and healing on behalf of_____ (insert clients name) may Reiki's infinite wisdom go exactly where it is needed most, should it be for their higher good. May we all be empowered by your divine love and blessing -Amen."

Cleanse and Harmonise Your Clients Aura

Prior to commencing the Reiki treatment run your hands in your clients aura about six inches above their body from their head right down to their feet in a slow smooth motion at least three times to remove any superficial energy build ups. This will also bring harmony to your client's aura and form a positive rapport between you and your client. Pay attention to your hands, use your intuition, sense for possible blockages or hot spots to focus on during your healing session. ***You are now ready to begin the treatment***.

If ye have faith as a grain of mustard seed, ye shall say unto this mountain, Remove hence to yonder place; and it shall remove - St. Matthew 17:20

10

Treating Others with Reiki

The only work that will ultimately bring any good to any of us is the work of contributing to the healing of the world. - Marianne Williamson

Before you begin a full body treatment on another person there are a few important points to remember.

Never give a Reiki treatment to a person who has a pacemaker as Reiki can alter its rhythm.

Never give a Reiki treatment to a person who suffers from Diabetes Mellitus and are taking insulin injections, unless they are prepared to check their insulin levels every day as Reiki reduces the amount of insulin they require.

Always explain to a person who is visiting you for the first time for a Reiki treatment exactly what you are going to do and the type of reactions that might occur. Stress that any one of these reactions are normal. They may experience one or two of these reactions, all of them or none of them. It makes no difference. Reiki will go wherever it is needed.

The types of reactions that may occur are:

- A sensation of heat
- A sensation of cold
- Recipient my see lots of colours often very vivid
- Past life flashes/recall
- Involuntary movements or mild spasms
- The recipient may become so relaxed they fall asleep
- Itchiness
- Emotional responses
- Rumbling stomach
- Memory flashes
- Pins and needles
- They recipient may sense your hands moving, even if you are not currently moving your hands from one hand position to another

Often the client will experience extreme cold at the position of your hands while you feel intense heat or vice versa; your client will experience heat while you feel cold.

If the client experiences nothing explain to them that the Reiki energy often works on a subtle level yet has profound results which normally become apparent in the following days or weeks.

Never forget the client is drawing Reiki through you. They are doing the healing on a subconscious level. You are only the channel.

Reiki always travels to the place it is needed most.

No knowledge of the human anatomy or physiology is required to work with Reiki. Leave your ego aside and Reiki will do the work.

Forget the symptoms treat the whole person.

Listen to your clients' body through your hands. Sense the different types of energy. If the energy is strong keep your hands in that position until your sense a shift in the energy level. Use your intuition.

Look for non-verbal communication from your clients' body. Deep sighs or hand and leg movements are good indicators that something positive is taking place.

The normal time required for a full body treatment is between sixty to ninety minutes.

At the end of a treatment always offer your client a glass of cold water to aid grounding. Always wash your hands under cold running water after each treatment.

Beginning The Treatment

Ensure your client is lying flat on the therapy table with their arms down by their sides. Their legs should also be flat against the table and must not be crossed as this may block the flow of Reiki.

Gently lay your hands on your clients' body. Keep them in each position for between three to five minutes. As you become more experienced use your intuition.

Your hands should be cupped with your fingers firmly closed as though you were trying to hold water. This keeps the channel strong between your client and the universal life force. If your fingers are open Reiki can escape just as water would slip through your open fingers.

In the case of burnt skin or a clients' genitals and breasts hold your hands just above their body.

Don't forget the box of tissues.

Full Body Treatment – Hand Positions

Remember the following hand positions are only a guide. Use your intuition!

Hand Position 1

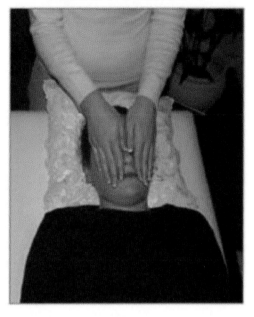

Cup your hands and gently rest them over your clients' eyes, cheekbones and forehead (third eye chakra).

Stress, eye problems, asthma, head colds, allergies, sinuses, pituitary gland, pineal gland and cerebral nerves.

Hand Position 2

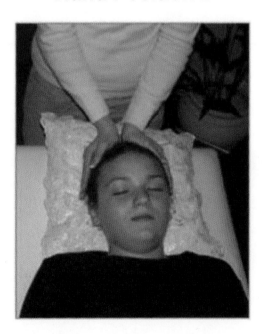

Place your hand on top of your clients' head; palms covering the crown chakra.

Migraine, headaches, eye problems, multiple sclerosis, stress, bladder, digestive disorders, flatulence and emotional problems.

Hand Position 3

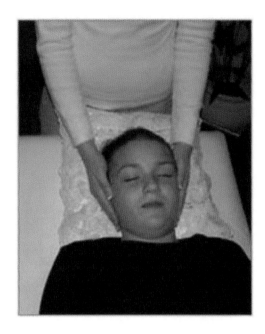

Hands on either side of your clients' head with fingers covering their temples.

Balance, tinnitus, balance and ear problems, colds, flu and balances the function of the right and left brain.

How To Move Your Hands From The Side

Of Your Clients' Head To Position 4

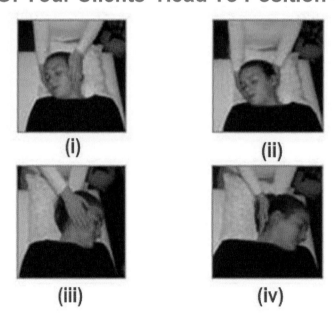

(i)   (ii)

(iii)   (iv)

Hand Position 4

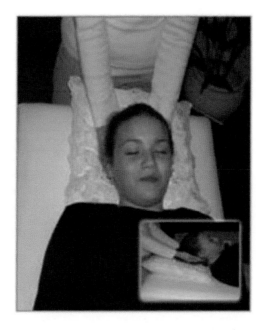

Place your hands on the back of your clients' head covering their occipital ridge.

Headaches, eye problems, stress, hay fever, sinuses, digestive disorders, fears, phobias, shock depression and stroke.

How To Move Your Hands From The Back
Of Your Clients' Head To Position 5

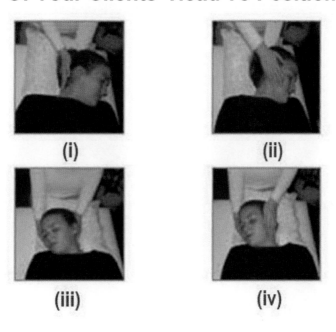

(i)   (ii)

(iii)   (iv)

Hand Position 5

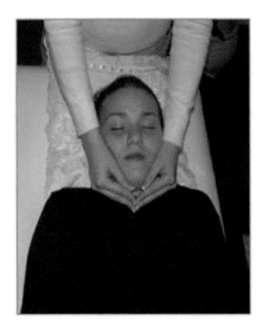

Place your hands along the clients' jawbone covering their throat chakra.

Self expression, communication, breathing, voice and speech problems, bronchitis, flu, colds and anger.

Hand Position 6

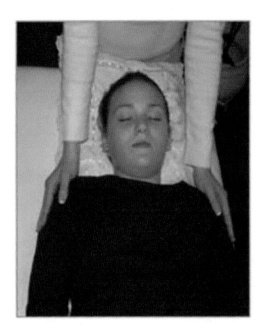

Place your hands along the clients' shoulders.

Aches and pains in the arms, elbows and hands, tight shoulder muscles, stress, cold hands, poor circulation or disrupted blood supply to the arms and hands.

Hand Positions 7-12

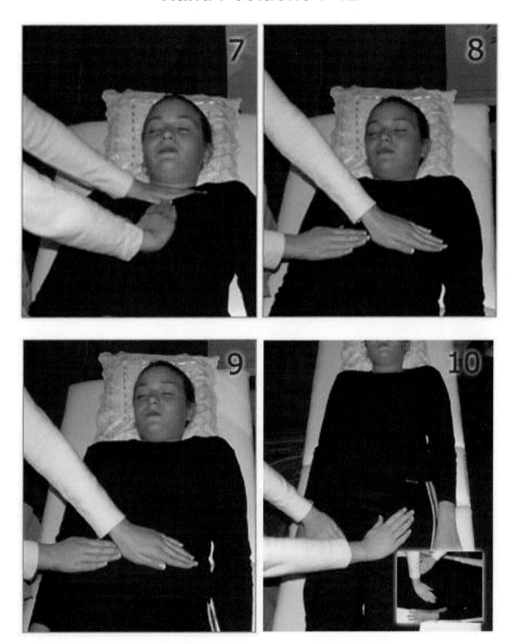

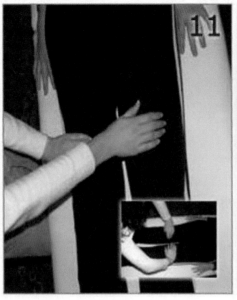 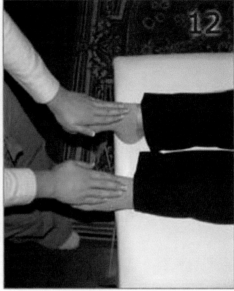

Begin by forming a T covering the collar bone and heart chakra (position 7). Then move your hands down the front and across the body covering the solar plexus and sacral chakra points (positions 8 and 9).

Form a V to cover the root chakra (position 10).

Finally, place your hands over your clients' knees and feet (positions 11 and 12).

All major organs and glands, disease, infections, stomach, intestines, reproductive organs, anger, stress, emotions, leg pains, varicose veins and poor circulation.

Now you have completed the front hand positions; ask your client to turn over so you can begin work on the back hand positions.

You may find that on occasions your client has fallen asleep and you will need to gently wake them up.

Hand Positions 13 – 19

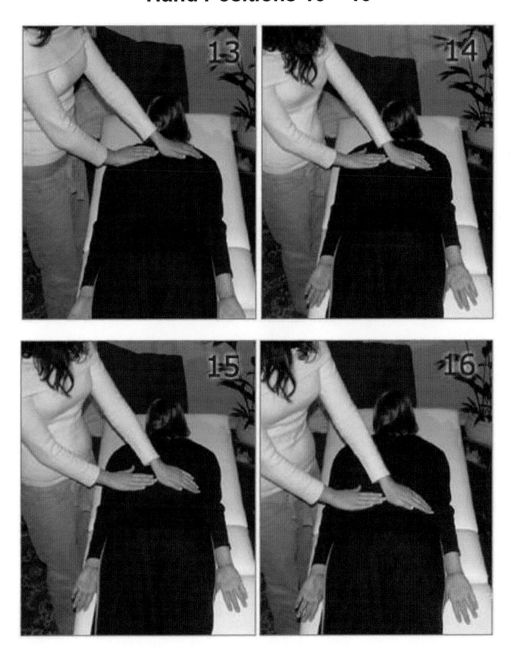

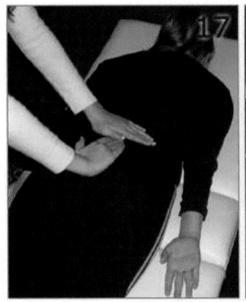
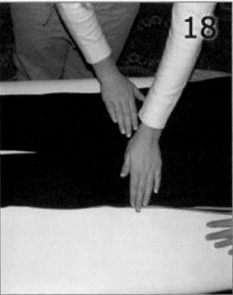
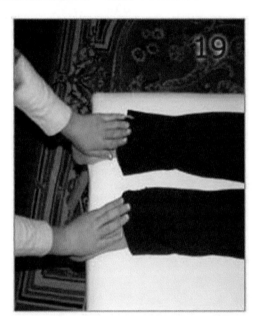

Begin by placing your hands across your client's shoulder blades (position 13). Then move your hands down their back covering the heart, solar plexus and sacral chakra points (positions 14, 15 and 16).

Form a T to cover the root chakra (position 17).

Finally, place your hands on the back of your clients' knees and feet (positions 18 and 19).

All major organs and glands, disease, infections, back and spinal problems, anger, stress, emotions, leg pains, varicose veins and poor circulation. You can also treat all major organs and glands through the reflexology points in your clients' feet.

Finally

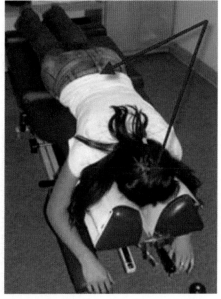

When all the positions have been treated, place your left hand on your clients crown chakra and your right hand at the base of their spine. This final position balances the energy in your clients' body.

Complete your treatment by combing your clients' aura. Stroke the body firmly from the crown down to the feet in a sweeping motion. Continue past the feet until you touch the floor for grounding. Repeat for a second time lightly touching the body. Finally comb the aura a few inches above the body.

Belief creates the actual fact. - William James

11

Rapid Reiki Treatment

The key to change... is to let go of fear. – Rosanne Cash

On many occasions you will find it's not practical to spend sixty to ninety minutes conducting a complete Reiki treatment. Often for numerous reasons the person needing Reiki has a limited amount of time or you simply are called into action in a place far away from your normal healing room.

There is an alternative quick and versatile technique that can be used in these situations. The Rapid Reiki treatment focuses on all the major chakra points while the client sits upright in a chair, and takes between fifteen to thirty minutes to complete.

Position 1

Your client should be seated in a straight back chair or stool. Stand behind your client with your hands on their shoulders.

Remember to take a moment to go inside, prepare for the healing session and recite your silent invocation.

Positions 2 – 3

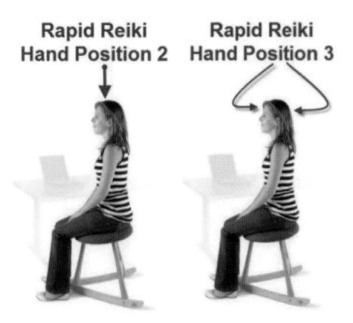

Rapid Reiki Hand Position 2

Rapid Reiki Hand Position 3

Position 2: Remain behind the Client and place both of your hands on top of their head covering their crown Chakra.

Position 3: Move to the side of your client and place one hand on their forehead and the other hand in the back of their head over their occipital ridge covering their 3rd eye chakra.

Positions 4 – 5

Rapid Reiki Hand Position 4

Rapid Reiki Hand Position 5

Position 4: Remaining at the side of your client; place one hand over the throat chakra and one hand at the back of the clients' neck.

Position 5: Remaining at the side of your client; Place one hand on the heart chakra and one hand at the back on their shoulder blades.

Positions 6 – 7

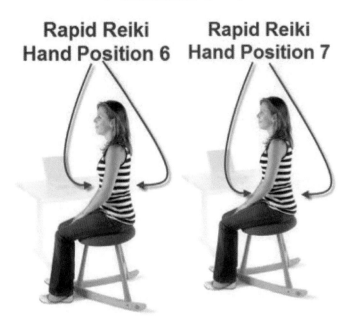

Rapid Reiki Hand Position 6   **Rapid Reiki Hand Position 7**

Position 6: Remaining at the side of your client; place one hand on your clients' solar plexus chakra and one hand at the back on their spine.

Position 7: Remaining at the side of your client; place one hand on your clients' sacral chakra and one hand at the back on their spine.

Positions 8 – 9

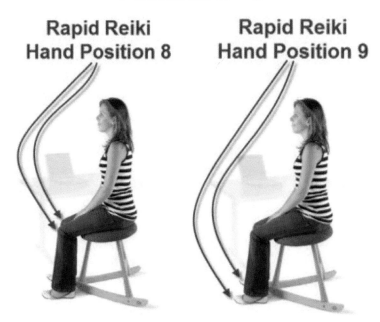

Rapid Reiki Hand Position 8   **Rapid Reiki Hand Position 9**

Position 8: Move to the front of your client; place one cupped hand on each of your clients' knees.

Position 9: Remaining at the front of your client; place one hand on each of your clients' feet.

Finally comb your client's aura three times as you normally would after a full treatment. Wash your hands in cold running water and offer a cold drink of water to your client to assist grounding.

Please Note: For your comfort positions 3 – 8 should be conducted while sitting in a chair or on a stool. Spend 3 – 5 minutes on each position unless your intuition tells you otherwise.

A little Reiki is better than no Reiki at all

I have no doubt whatever that most people live, whether physically, intellectually, or morally, in a very restricted circle of their potential being. They make use of a very small portion of their possible consciousness, and of their soul's resources in general, much like a man who, out of his whole bodily organism, should get into a habit of using only his little finger. Great emergencies and crises show us how much greater our vital resources are than we had supposed…. We all have reservoirs of life to draw upon, of which we do not dream. – William James

Happiness resides not in possessions; and not in gold, happiness dwells in the soul. – Democritus

12

The Ultradian Rhythm Technique

Health is the greatest possession. Contentment is the greatest treasure.
Confidence is the greatest friend. Non-being is the greatest joy. - Lao Tzu

What is the Ultradian Rhythm?

Biological research has discovered that the human body functions in various cycles. One of these cycles is the ultradian rhythm; the natural body cycle of activity and rest. During sleep we dream every 90-120 minutes, even if we do not remember doing so. In our daily lives this rhythm continues. During the day we often have a sudden urge to stop and rest. The body needs to take short breaks every 90-120 minutes to repair and maintain itself.

THE ULTRADIAN PERFORMANCE RHYTHM

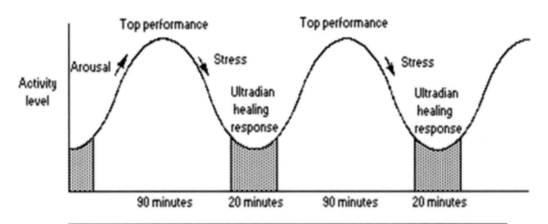

Adapted from: Rossi, EL: The 20 Minute Break. Tarcher-Putnam, New York, 1991, p. 12.

Most people misjudge this natural and important process and fail to allow themselves a short power break. Instead of relaxing and recharging their batteries most people opt for a quick boost of energy. This normally comes in the form of a coffee or tea break, sweets, chocolates, fizzy drinks or cigarettes. Unfortunately all of these are stimulants and simply gloss over the underlying need of the body to take regular breaks if it to maintain health and well-being. When we consistently ignore these essential psycho-physiological breaks we are upsetting the fine balance and rhythms of the mind body and spirit.

This neglect leads to health problems and stress related disorders such as depression, mood swings, psychosomatic pain and illnesses, sexual dysfunction, eating disorders and a wide variety of psychological problems. Reiki can be used to prevent and help treat this problem by bringing the body back in to equilibrium and normalising the Ultradian rhythm.

The Ultradian Rhythm Technique

During the day look out for signs from your body-mind telling you to stop for a moment and rest. These signs normally manifest as a sudden feeling of slowing down or loss of energy. You may feel yourself drift off into a semi-trance like state, somewhat like daydreaming.

At this point allow yourself a short break and you will revitalise and rejuvenate your whole mind body and spirit. Place your cupped hands over your eyes as shown in the image below (self healing hand position 1). Close your eyes and go inside.

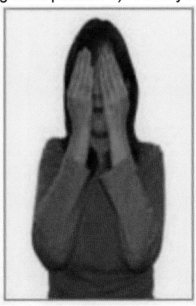

Become aware of any part of your body that feels tight, sore or tired. If you discover a part of your body that you sense or feel needs reiki move your hands to that place on your body and keep them there for as long as you need in order for the pain or discomfort to dissipate. Try to imagine or sense that part of your body being filled with a vivid healing white light – Reiki.

Then make the light grow brighter and brighter, larger and larger until it envelopes your whole body mind and spirit. Sense the feeling of peace and well being as the healing white light fills your aura and forms a protective shield of pure unconditional love and healing invigorating energy around you. When you feel rejuvenated and recharged gently open your eyes and continue with your day.

Repeat this exercise on a regular basis to keep your energy levels high and to prevent stress and ill health. It is really important to change how you respond to this natural rhythm of life. Replace the junk food and quick attempts to boost your energy levels with this healthier and natural self healing technique that will add years to your life.

If you fail to find a part of the body that needs reiki during this exercise; go back inside once more and look again. Often we have found it takes a second or even third look inside to find a part of the body that requires healing. This is because it is invariably hidden deep inside the unconscious mind. However, if you fail to uncover anything simply keep your hands over your eyes for as long as you require. The short break will still be beneficial to your health and well being.

When time or conditions prevent you taking these short power breaks, there is another simple way of maintaining your fight against fatigue, sickness and disease. The thymus gland which is situated between the throat and the heart chakra (see illustration below) is a twin lobed organ that is responsible for producing white infection fighting blood cells. Although the functions of the thymus are not fully understood, it is known to play a part in the development of immunities against various diseases by forming a hormone essential to the immune system known as THF (thymic humoral factor).

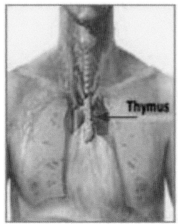

Researchers believe that it is this hormone that acts on lymphocytes, causing them to change into plasma cells, which subsequently form antibodies that produce immunities.

Tap gently 20-30 times on your chest over the position of the thymus (see illustration above) or place one of your hands over the position for several minutes. This simple technique will help maintain and boost your immune system while filling your body, mind and spirit with vitality.

*Judge each day not by the harvest you reap
but by the seeds you plant. - Robert Louis Stevenson*

13

Group Reiki Treatment

Love and desire are the spirit's wings to great deeds. - Johann Wolfgang von Goethe

Group treatments were first used by Dr Hayashi at his clinic in Tokyo. He would often treat clients with the help of several other Reiki practitioners. Many people find it more enjoyable to work with another person or persons. There are also several advantages to working in a group.

The Benefits of Group Treatment

Group Treatment is quicker taking as little as six to ten minutes to complete a full Reiki treatment.

Group Treatment is very powerful. The client receives an intense burst of healing energy. This often has the effect of kick starting the clients' natural healing process.

Group Treatment allows the team to form a bond and create a unique energy. As we all experience Reiki in different ways, clients will often notice the different energy vibrations from different Reiki practitioners.

Group Treatments | Front Hand Positions

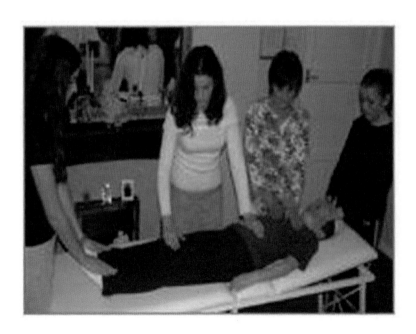

Group Treatments | Back Hand Positions

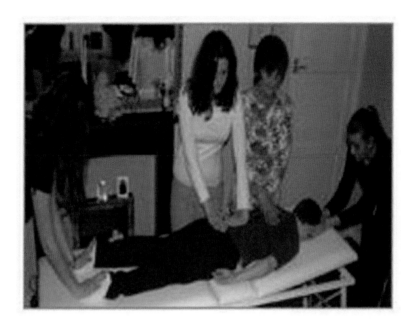

Guidelines for Conducting a Group Treatment

All the normal preparations and procedures of a full Reiki treatment still apply to a group session.

Before you begin a group treatment decide who will work on the head positions and ultimately control the healing session.

Depending on how many Reiki practitioners are involved in the group treatment decide who will work on the various hand positions. Don't forget to decide who will complete the session by smoothing the clients aura.

If four or more practitioners are taking part in the healing session you can have one practitioner at each end of the clients' body while the other practitioners work in the middle.

Remember to have a box of tissues available.

This is a wonderful way to treat many people in a short space of time and ideal for therapy days. However, remember to wash your hands before and after each treatment under cold running water to dissipate any negative energy and assist grounding for each member of the team.

Spend time sharing experiences. Group treatment is a great way to learn and grow together.

Look within. Within is the fountain of good, and it will ever bubble up, if thou wilt ever dig. - Marcus Aurelius

14

Reiki and Pregnancy, Babies and Children

Nothing is impossible; the word itself says 'I'm possible'! - Audrey Hepburn

Pregnancy

Reiki is both safe and extremely beneficial to an unborn child and their pregnant mother. We have found that women who have studied the first degree and are attuned to the universal life force find the experience of pregnancy and childbirth more enjoyable and easier to cope with. Reiki can help during pregnancy in various ways such as:

Reiki alleviates morning sickness.

Reiki helps reduce stress and tiredness.

Reiki stimulates the babies' healthy development.

Reiki can be used to treat painful muscles, joints or the spine.

Reiki strengthens the bond between a mother and her baby. When a mother who is attuned to Reiki places her hands on her tummy she is passing pure unconditional love and healing to her unborn child.

Reiki keeps the mind body and spirit in balance reducing the chances of post natal depression.

Reiki nourishes the foetus with love and the universal life force. It gently comforts, protects and envelops the unborn baby.

If the father of an unborn baby is a Reiki practitioner he can also help during the pregnancy by treating his partner. The important bond between father and child will also be stimulated each time he places his hands on his partners' pregnant tummy. The father can communicate through his hands with his child.

Reiki can help couples who are finding it difficult to conceive a child by reducing stress and stimulating both the females' natural reproductive cycle and the males' production of sperm. In many cases when a couple are desperate for a child they place extreme stress on themselves causing an imbalance of their mind body and spirits. So often the moment they give up and forget about trying to have children, and the pressure and stress factor is removed many couples find their prayers are answered and a pregnancy is discovered.

Babies

Reiki can accelerate the recovery time of the mother and baby after the birth. It is especially good for caesareans sections and healing the various scars and stitches often associated with childbirth.

Reiki can be used to heal the babies' umbilical cord.

Reiki can be used to vitalised and nourish the mother's milk if the baby is breast feed. Alternatively, if the baby is to be bottled feed the formula can be treated with Reiki. Treating and enriching the babies food can help nourish and satisfy the babies hunger. This will help them suckle until they are content and full. Regular filling feeds lead to less sleepless nights. Something all parents pray for.

Reiki stimulates balance in the new born baby. It can easily be channelled to the baby whenever the mother or father (depending on who has been attuned to the energy) touches their child.

Reiki can be used to help treat cradle cap, colic and wind.

Important Note: Always consult your doctor no matter how trivial it may seem if you are concerned about your baby.

Children

Reiki can be used to treat your children throughout their lives. From the early days and months through puberty, adolescence and into adulthood.

Reiki is wonderful for all their aches and pains. Instinctively we touch or kiss our children better when they fall or injure themselves. With Reiki we speed up the healing process and boost their own natural healing abilities.

Reiki is a special gift you can share with your children. We recommend you teach your own children the five principles of Reiki and have them incorporate them into their lives.

Children love Reiki. If possible you should introduce and attune your children to Reiki. It will help them focus and find their own path in life.

Use Reiki at bedtime to help your children drift off to sleep.

Reiki balances your child's mind body and spirit leading to a clearer more focussed approach to life at school and at home.

When a child has an accident they often cry because of the shock. Treat your child by placing one of your hands on their solar plexus and the other at the base of the spine.

There are two ways of spreading light: to be the candle
or the mirror that reflects it. - Edith Wharton

15

Reiki Brings Comfort to Those Souls Crossing Over

Death is not the greatest loss in life. The greatest loss is what dies inside us while we live. - Norman Cousins

There is only one certainty in life and that is that death comes to us all. Facing our own mortality is often difficult. We have two main choices in coming to terms with our own death or the death of a family member or friend. We can choose to view death as final and become consumed in grief or we can envisage life after death and celebrate the transition to eternal life. Our beliefs and personal experiences shape how we deal with this extremely emotive issue.

Losing my sister Kim at the young age of thirty-three was a devastating blow to both me and my family. It was the first time I had experienced losing someone close. Looking back in hindsight and through my own research and subsequent experiences with people who came to me for help before dying, I found many common attitudes and mistakes associated with death. The western world in general treats the subject of dying as taboo. Something we shouldn't talk about.

As a stark contrast, Eastern philosophy and the teachings and beliefs of many ancient cultures view death as a natural part of life. They believe that our souls are eternal. The body is only a temporary vessel that allows the soul access to Earth. Karmicly we are here to learn and grow.

When a person becomes more spiritually aware they grow to understand and accept these ancient beliefs. When you look at the two choices it should be easy to believe in life after death, rather than believe that death is final and we all have nothing else to look forward to. All religions are built on the premise that to obtain eternal life you must be good in this one.

Thanatology (the study of death and the dying) has giving humanity the insight into life after death. People who have had near death experiences bring hope and reports of a better place. Books such as Saved By The Light by Dannion Brinkley offer inspiration and comfort to us all.

In 1975 Dannion was struck by lightning as he made a telephone call to a business partner during a thunderstorm. He was pronounced dead in the ambulance on the way to hospital. For a little over twenty minutes he experienced what many people fear the most — **what really happens to you when you die**.

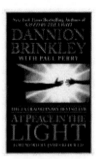

Dannion Brinkley tells how his ethereal soul leaves his earthly body and floats high above looking down at the scene of his death. He felt no pain or sadness at leaving his body or his life behind. A tunnel of bright light appears in front of him and he is quickly engulfed by it.

As he progresses into the light he feels an overwhelming sense of peace and love. He goes on to tell of meeting spiritual beings and being shown a beautiful spiritual realm.

This life changing experience is not unique to Dannion Brinkley; thousands of other people who have died on the operating table or after an accident only to come back from the brink have reported similar experiences.

If Dannion had been the only person to profess to such a profound experience then we could dismiss it as fiction or fantasy. A man with a wild imagination who suffered hallucinations; perhaps after a serious and almost fatal accident.

There are nine common traits that thanatologists like Dr Raymond Moody (author of life after life) have been able to define through countless studies with people who have had near death experiences. This research proves there is life after death. The nine common traits are as follows:

A person senses they are dead.

A feeling of peace without pain no matter how they died.

An out of body experience. Their soul or essence floats above the dead body below.

A tunnel appears and the person is drawn into another world.

Beings of light appear often deceased relatives and friends.

A particular being of light appears to greet and guide them.

The being of light takes them through a life review which highlights all the pleasant and unpleasant aspects of their life.

The person is told they must return. They feel reluctant to do so but understand they have no choice.

On returning the person has a personality transformation. They no longer fear death and are often guided and inspired towards a new definite purpose in their life.

The knowledge that there is life after death should be incorporated into your own life as well as the life of your family, friends and people who you meet along your path to eternal life. We urge you to study and become more aware of how to use this knowledge to help people who fear death. Make their transition a happy and joyous experience. Treat also their families so they may celebrate in the knowledge that their love-ones are not suffering and lost forever. They have simply migrated to a beautiful spiritual world that is filled with pure unconditional love. One day they will once again meet and be with them.

Working With People Who Are Dying

Reiki connects us to the universal life force; the energy and unconditional love that people who have had near death experiences talk about. When you use Reiki in a situation such as with a person who is terminally ill you are connecting them to the unconditional love of God and preparing them for their transition. You will often find Reiki temporarily revitalises them so they have the energy to deal with any unfinished business they may have.

It is important to help them if possible tidy up their affairs. Teach them to heal and mend any family relationships that may have been strained in the past. Encourage them to forgive and let go of any unnecessary anger and pain. **Death is not failure it is a natural part of life**. Encourage family members and friends to say goodbye and let the person who is dying know it's okay to go, and although it hurts they can survive and carry on without them. This often brings relief and removes the feeling of guilt from the person who is dying.

Reiki can alleviate pain and anxiety and bring final peace and harmony to the mind body and spirit. Reiki gives the person control of how and when they die. **Reiki builds a bridge to the other side** and brings the life of the person to a joyful conclusion.

Treat the family and friends if possible with Reiki after their love-one has passed on. We have found while the soul has departed and gone on to a joyous beginning the people left behind often find it extremely difficult to come to terms with losing a close family member or friend. Heal their pain and fill their mind body spirit and lives with the unconditional and omnipotent love of Reiki.

When you were born, you cried and the world rejoiced. Live your life
in such a manner that when you die, the world cries
and you rejoice. - Traditional Indian Saying

16

Use Your Imagination

Can you imagine what I would do if I could do all I can? - Sun Tzu

Reiki is present in all living things. Your imagination is the only thing that can set limitations on its uses.

We have listed some of the most common in this lesson.

Reiki and Animals

All animals adore Reiki; large or small, fierce or friendly. Animals are extremely sensitive to the healing energy of Reiki. Start practising with your own pets and as you become more confident you can move onto other people's pets and animals. As with treating humans; Reiki will go where it is needed most. The only difference with animals is that they often guide you to the exact place that requires treatment by moving around until your hand lands on the exact spot. Animals will also let you know when they have had enough by moving away.

There is a huge market for treating animals. Use your imagination to develop your own techniques for treatment and develop a marketing strategy. Talk to your local vet or animal welfare centre. Advertise; you'll be surprised at the number of people with pets who need and want your help.

Basic Techniques for Animals:

The very small animals such as birds or mice can be cupped in your hands.

Larger animals such as cats, dogs, horses and cows normally prefer you to begin by placing your hands behind their ears and working around the body as with a normal full treatment for humans. However, if the animal has a specific injury; place your hands directly over the injury.

Fish can be treated by placing your hands on either side of the fish tank.

Animals that are wild or dangerous can be treated safely through distance healing (second degree).

Another safe way to treat animals is by treating their food and drink. However, this is a weaker form of treatment.

REMEMBER USE YOUR IMAGINATION

Plants and Vegetation

Reiki will enrich your plants, flowers, trees and gardens. Daily treatment will soon show positive results. The easiest way to prove how effective Reiki is with your plants and vegetation is to conduct a simple experiment.

Take several seeds, charge half of them with Reiki and place them in a pot. Then plant the other untreated seeds in a separate identical pot. Treat the seeds which were charged in the beginning with Reiki each day and observe how they flourish. Compare them to the pot of seeds that are simply left to grow naturally.

Basic Techniques for Plants and Vegetation

Treat seeds or bulbs before sowing or planting by cupping them in your hands for several minutes.

Indoor and outdoor potted plants can be treated daily by placing your hands around the pot.

Flowers, bushes and plants can be treated by placing your hands gently on their leaves, buds, branches or stems.

Hold cut flowers by their stems for a couple of minutes. Continue daily treatment by placing your hands around the vase and you will extend the flowers life.

Trees need longer treatments. The easiest way is to hug a tree.

Lawns, plants, shrubs, flowers and trees can also be treated by treating their water supply.

Larger gardens, woods and forests can be treated through distance healing (second degree).

Food and Drink

Treat your food and drink before you consume it. This will enrich it with the universal life force and improve the digestion process. The consumption of food takes more energy than any other bodily function. The quicker and more easily it is digested the more energy is available for other activities.

Basic Techniques for Food and Drink

If you grow your own vegetables and herbs treat as shown previously for plants and vegetation.

During food preparation you can place the food in your hands and conduct a short Reiki treatment. This is especially good if you are preparing a meal for the family.

Just before you eat or drink place your hands just above the plate or glass. This is especially useful if you are eating out, and are unable to see the food being prepared.

Alternatively you can place your hands on your stomach to assist digestion.

Further Uses for Reiki

There are a million and one other uses for Reiki including:

Flat car batteries, especially on cold winter mornings.

The medicine cabinet or first aid box.

The Bath water.

Your Home, your car.

Protection while travelling on trains, planes, buses etc.

Your work, letters, documents.

In fact you are only limited by your imagination!

Use Your Imagination Right Now By Listing As Many Ideas As You Can On Different Ways To Use Reiki In Your Life. Then Make Sure And Try Them Out. Each Idea Will Breed Another. Have Fun…. Good Luck.

I saw the angel in the marble and carved until I set him free. – Michelangelo

17

Final Thoughts

*"My interest is in the future because I am going to spend
the rest of my life there" – Charles F. Kettering*

The first degree is the beginning of a wonderful journey filled with learning and growth on so many different levels. Many people find that the first degree is all they need to study and incorporate, to lead a more fulfilling life.

While others, will continue their studies and progress onto the second degree and then master/teacher degree.

The first degree connects the student to the universal life force and gives them the tools to heal themselves, their family and others.

Many people just like ourselves, have been drawn to Reiki and find that it changes their lives for the better. Reiki brings a sense of purpose, knowledge direction, calm and equilibrium into a chaotic world.

We have been able to incorporate the principles and teachings of Reiki into our personal lives and into our clinical practice entwining its energy and philosophy seamlessly into the other disciplines, practices and treatments we work with.

Reiki combines extremely well with all other therapies, including reflexology; aromatherapy, massage, the metamorphic technique, hypnosis, hypnotherapy, gestalt therapy, NLP, Dream work, regression therapy, focusing and crystal healing to name but a few.

It also combines safely with orthodox medical care, particularly post-operatively health care, helping to accelerate the natural healing process.

Reiki is a special gift to be cherished and used. We urge you to incorporate Reiki into your lives and use this gift daily or as often as possible. Get busy and heal yourself, your family, your friends and others.

Life is an adventure. Live it! Enjoy it!

Congratulations on Completing Your Study of Reiki Level 1

We would like to congratulate you on completing the **Essence of Reiki 1** – our manual which we use in our Certified Usui Reiki Practitioner workshops and Home Study Courses.

We are both honoured and blessed that we have been able to guide you along this spiritual path to a new future filled with the power, beauty and wonder of Reiki. We hope you will embrace Reiki into your life and allow it to envelope and inspire you in your future.

Love and Light

Garry & Adele Malone

Reiki Master/Teachers Since 1997

If you would like more information about our Certified Usui Reiki Home Study courses please visit http://reiki-store.co.uk to discover how you can become a Certified Usui Reiki Master Teacher.

If you would like more information about our Reiki Practice Development Home Study courses please visit http://reiki-store.com and discover how we can help mentor and guide you build a thriving reiki practice.

Printed in Great Britain
by Amazon.co.uk, Ltd.,
Marston Gate.